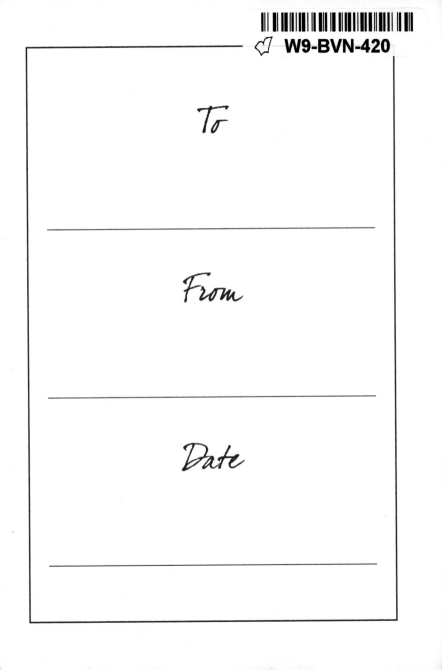

W9-BVN-420

To

From

Date

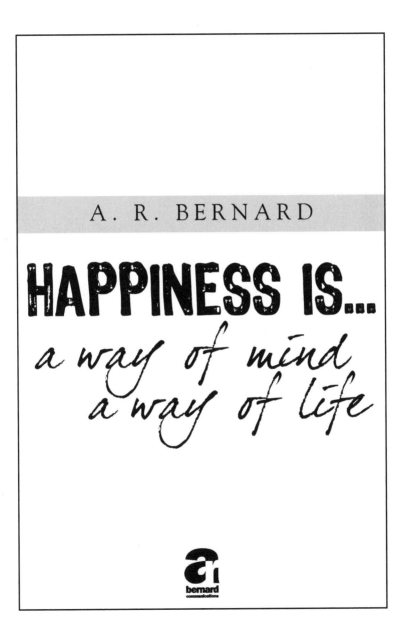

A. R. BERNARD

# HAPPINESS IS...

*a way of mind*
*a way of life*

bernard
communications

A.R. Bernard Enterprises LLC
P.O. Box 781
Smithtown, New York 11787
info@arbernard.com

*The quoted ideas expressed in this book (but not scripture verses) are not, in all cases, exact quotations, as some have been edited for clarity and brevity. In all cases, the author has attempted to maintain the speaker's original intent. In some cases, quoted material for this book was obtained from secondary sources, primarily print media. While every effort was made to ensure the accuracy of these sources, the accuracy cannot be guaranteed. For additions, deletions, corrections or clarifications in future editions of this text, please write A.R. Bernard Enterprises LLC.*

Scripture quotations are taken from:

The Holy Bible, King James Version (KJV)

The Holy Bible, New International Version (NIV) Copyright © 1973, 1978, 1984, by International Bible Society. Used by permission of Zondervan Publishing House. All rights reserved.

The New American Standard Bible®, (NASB) Copyright © 1960, 1962, 1963, 1968, 1971, 1972, 1973, 1975, 1977, 1995 by The Lockman Foundation. Used by permission.

The Holy Bible, New King James Version (NKJV) Copyright © 1982 by Thomas Nelson, Inc. Used by permission.

The Holy Bible, New Living Translation, (NLT) Copyright © 1996. Used by permission of Tyndale House Publishers, Inc., Wheaton, Illinois 60189. All rights reserved.

New Century Version®. (NCV) Copyright © 1987, 1988, 1991 by Word Publishing, a division of Thomas Nelson, Inc. All rights reserved. Used by permission.

The Holy Bible: Revised Standard Version (RSV). Copyright 1946, 1952, 1959, 1973 by the Division of Christian Education of the National Council of the Churches of Christ in the United States of America. All rights reserved. Used by permission.

The Holy Bible, The Living Bible (TLB), Copyright © 1971 owned by assignment by Illinois Regional Bank N.A. (as trustee). Used by permission of Tyndale House Publishers, Inc., Wheaton, Illinois 60189. All rights reserved.

The Message (MSG) This edition issued by contractual arrangement with NavPress, a division of The Navigators, U.S.A. Originally published by NavPress in English as THE MESSAGE: The Bible in Contemporary Language copyright 2002-2003 by Eugene Peterson. All rights reserved.

International Children's Bible®, New Century Version®. (ICB) Copyright © 1986, 1988, 1999 by Tommy Nelson™, a division of Thomas Nelson, Inc. All rights reserved. Used by permission.

The Holman Christian Standard Bible™ (HOLMAN CSB) Copyright © 1999, 2000, 2001 by Holman Bible Publishers. Used by permission.

Cover Design by Kim Russell / Wahoo Designs
Page Layout by Bart Dawson

ISBN 1-58334-390-3

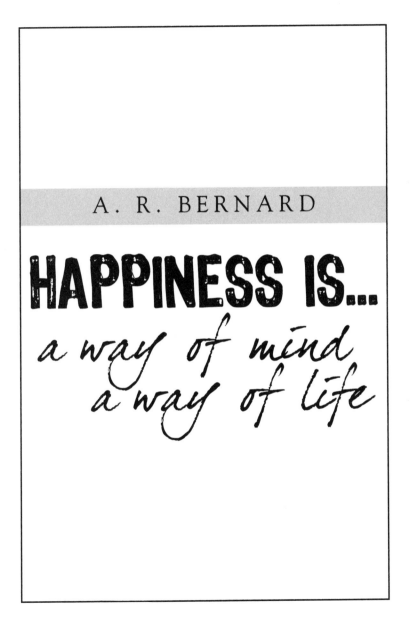

A. R. BERNARD

# HAPPINESS IS...

*a way of mind*
*a way of life*

# Table of Contents

# *Introduction*

I n the spring of 2004, I read an article in *USA Today* by Kevin Maney entitled "Money Can't Buy Happiness, But Happiness May Buy Money." In it, Mr. Maney summarized some impressive research findings that demonstrate—just like you've heard all your life but may not have really believed—that cash *cannot* buy contentment. The article gave me the idea for a series of sermons on what happiness is—and what it isn't. This book is an extension of those sermons.

Now, I know what you're probably thinking: "A big stash of cash may not be able to buy me happiness, but I'd sure like the opportunity to find out for myself!" And if that's what you're thinking, then you're no different than billions of people around the globe. We human beings are quick to equate money with happiness, no matter how many times we hear otherwise.

Yet the research shows time and again that money, in and of itself, simply does not make folks happy. Don't believe me? Well here's a statistic to think about: Even though the average American's income has tripled (in buying power) since 1956, the number of Americans who say they're happy has stayed about the same, at around 30%. So if more money can't purchase contentment for the average American, then you're smart if you *don't* depend upon the "almighty" dollar as your primary tool for becoming a genuinely happy person.

But if money doesn't win happiness, what does? Genuine happiness is a way of mind and a way of life. Happiness results from the way you choose to interpret events and the choices you make as a result of those interpretations. If you choose to view the world in a positive way, if you work hard to achieve positive results, and if you associate with positive people, then you'll increase your odds of being happy (most of the time). But if you refuse to look at the donut and focus instead upon the hole, you can make yourself unhappy (most of the time) even if you've got a bigger bank balance than Bill Gates.

Happiness also depends upon your willingness to be a disciplined person, a person who is focused on doing *what* needs to be done *when* it needs to be done. Happiness depends upon your willingness to lead a purposeful, principled life. And, of course, your happiness depends upon the nature and the quality of your relationship with God.

This book is intended to help you explore happiness: what it means, how to find it, and how to keep it. So during the next 30 days, try this experiment: read a chapter each day and spend a few minutes thinking about the things you've read. Then, apply the lessons you've learned to the ups and downs of everyday life. When you do, you'll discover that happiness isn't a commodity that can be purchased in a store; it's a byproduct of the way you choose to live and the things you choose to think.

The ideas on these pages can—and should—be woven into the fabric of your life. Your life story is being written one day at a time . . . and with God's help, that story can—and will—be a masterpiece.

# HAPPINESS IS...

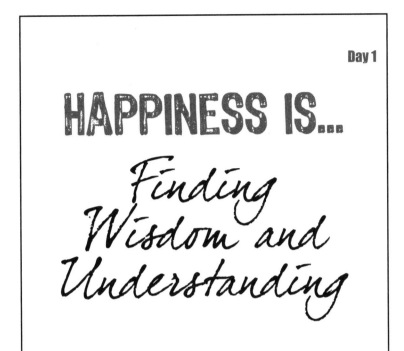

*Finding Wisdom and Understanding*

*Happy is the person who finds wisdom
and gains understanding.*

Proverbs 3:13 NLT

Happiness begins with wisdom and understanding. In other words, happiness and wisdom are traveling companions. But here's a word of warning: the acquisition of wisdom is seldom easy or quick.

Wisdom is not like a mushroom; it does not spring up overnight. It is, instead, like an oak tree that starts as a tiny acorn, grows into a sapling, and eventually reaches up to the sky, tall and strong.

Do you seek wisdom? Then seek it every day of your life. Seek it with consistency and purpose. And, seek it in the right place. That place, of course, is, first and foremost, the Word of God.

Sometimes, amid the demands of daily life, you will lose perspective. Life may seem out of balance, and the pressures of everyday living may seem overwhelming. What's needed is a fresh perspective, a restored sense of balance . . . and God's wisdom. If you call upon the Lord and seek to see the world through His eyes, He will give you guidance and perspective. If you make God's priorities your priorities, He will lead you along a path of His choosing. If you study God's teachings, you will be reminded that God's reality is the ultimate reality.

> The fear of the LORD is the beginning of wisdom, and the knowledge of the Holy One is understanding.
>
> Proverbs 9:10 NKJV

As you accumulate wisdom, you may feel the need to share your insights with friends and family members. If so, remember this: your actions must reflect the values that you hold dear. The best way to share your wisdom—perhaps the only way—is not by your words, but by your example.

So if you're really interested in being a happier person, then you must make up your mind to become a wiser person. It's the only way.

## Great Ideas About...
# Wisdom

The wisest mind has something yet to learn.

*George Santayana*

Follow your instincts.
That is where true wisdom manifests itself.

*Oprah Winfrey*

Knowledge is horizontal. Wisdom is vertical;
it comes down from above.

*Billy Graham*

No one is truly happy if he has what he wants,
but only if he wants something he should have.

*St. Augustine*

*Therefore everyone who hears these words of mine*
*and puts them into practice is like a wise man*
*who built his house on the rock.*

*Jesus, Matthew 7:24 NIV*

*But the wisdom that is from above is first pure, then peaceable,*
*gentle, willing to yield, full of mercy and good fruits,*
*without partiality and without hypocrisy.*

*James 3:17 NKJV*

## Today's Tip

Wisdom isn't just knowing what to do—
it's doing what you know.

*Your Thoughts*

# HAPPINESS IS...

*Living in the Now*

*This is the day the L{ORD} has made;*
*let us rejoice and be glad in it.*

Psalm 118:24 Holman CSB

All too often, people think of happiness as something that has already happened (in the distant past) or something that may occur "some day" (in the distant future)—but they're mistaken. Happiness, if it occurs at all, occurs in the present tense; happiness takes place in the precious present.

Are you willing to celebrate your life today? You should. After all, this day is a blessed gift from God. And when you stop to think about it, you probably have countless reasons to rejoice. Yet on some days, when the demands of life threaten to overwhelm you, you may not feel much like rejoicing. Instead of celebrating God's gifts, you may find yourself frustrated by the obligations of today and worried by the uncertainties of tomorrow. If so, it's time to redirect your thoughts to things positive . . . and it's time to start counting your blessings.

> *For he says,*
> *"In the time of my favor*
> *I heard you, and in*
> *the day of salvation*
> *I helped you." I tell you,*
> *now is the time of*
> *God's favor, now is*
> *the day of salvation.*
> 2 Corinthians 6:2 NIV

The familiar words of Psalm 118:24 remind us that this is the day the Lord has made, and we should rejoice. So whatever this day holds for you, begin it and end it with God as your partner. And throughout the day, give thanks to the One who created you. God's love for you is infinite. Accept it joyfully . . . and be happy. Now.

## Great Ideas About...
# Living in the Present

The present is holy ground.

*Alfred North Whitehead*

Whatever I'm doing, I don't think in terms of tomorrow.
I try to live in the present moment.

*Anita Baker*

Exhaust the little moment. Soon it dies.

*Gwendolyn Brooks*

I depend on the integrity and the faithfulness of God
to make each moment as meaningful as He can and as I allow.

*Bill Bright*

People create success in their lives by focusing on today.
It may sound trite, but today is the only time you have.
It's too late for yesterday. And you can't depend on tomorrow.

*John Maxwell*

*Since everything here today might well be gone tomorrow,*
*do you see how essential it is to live a holy life?*

2 Peter 3:11 MSG

*While it is daytime, we must continue doing the work of the One*
*who sent me. Night is coming, when no one can work.*

John 9:4 NCV

### Today's Tip

If you had to be the person you are today for the rest of your life,
would you be happy? If the answer is "Absolutely!" keep up
the good work. But if the answer is "Maybe"—or, for that
matter, an outright "No"—then it's time to take responsibility
for your future . . . and it's time to start making changes now.

*Your Thoughts*

# HAPPINESS IS...

## A Way of Mind

Finally brothers, whatever is true, whatever is honorable, whatever is just, whatever is pure, whatever is lovely, whatever is commendable—if there is any moral excellence and if there is any praise—dwell on these things.

*Philippians 4:8 Holman CSB*

imply put, happiness is a way of thinking. So here's the big question: How will you direct your thoughts today? Will you obey the words of Philippians 4:8 by dwelling upon those things that are honorable, true, and worthy of praise? Or will you allow your thoughts to be hijacked by the negativity that seems to dominate our troubled world?

Are you fearful, angry, bored, or worried? Are you so preoccupied with the concerns of this day that you fail to thank God for the promise of eternity? Are you confused, bitter, or pessimistic? If so, God wants to have a little talk with you.

God intends that you be an ambassador for Him, an enthusiastic, hope-filled Christian. But God won't force you to adopt a positive attitude. It's up to you to think positively about your blessings and opportunities . . . or not. So, today and every day hereafter, celebrate this life that God has given you by focusing your thoughts and your energies upon "things that are excellent and worthy of praise." Today, count your blessings instead of your hardships. And thank the Giver of all things good for gifts that are simply too numerous to count.

> Guard your heart
> above all else,
> for it is the source of life.
> Proverbs 4:23 Holman CSB

## Great Ideas About...
# Thoughts

Happiness doesn't depend upon who you are or what you have;
it depends upon what you think.

*Dale Carnegie*

The greater part of our happiness or misery depends
on our dispositions, and not our circumstances.

*Martha Washington*

Every good thought you think is contributing its share
to the ultimate result of your life.

*Grenville Kleiser*

I am happy and content because I think I am.

*Alain*

Our lives are what our thoughts make them.

*Marcus Aurelius*

*So prepare your minds for service and have self-control.*

1 Peter 1:13 NCV

*Those who are pure in their thinking are happy,*
*because they will be with God.*

Matthew 5:8 NCV

## Today's Tip

Happiness is a positive interpretation of the world and its events. Happiness requires that you train yourself to see the good in everything, no matter what happens.

*Your Thoughts*

# HAPPINESS IS...

## Love

And now abide faith, hope, love, these three;
but the greatest of these is love.

1 Corinthians 13:13 NKJV

Happiness means gaining an awareness of the tremendously positive power of love. And if there's anything that Jesus brought to this world, it was an awareness of the transformational power of love.

Love is a choice. Either you choose to behave lovingly toward others . . . or not; either you behave yourself in ways that enhance your relationships . . . or not. But make no mistake: genuine love requires effort. If you want to build relationships that last, you must be willing to do your part.

> Love other people
> just as Christ loved us.
>
> *Ephesians 5:2 ICB*

Since the days of Adam and Eve, God has allowed His children to make choices for themselves, and so it is with you. As you interact with family and friends, you have choices to make . . . lots of them. If you choose wisely, you'll be happier and healthier; if you choose unwisely, you'll bear the consequences.

God does not intend for you to experience mediocre relationships; He created you for far greater things. Building lasting relationships requires compassion, wisdom, empathy, kindness, courtesy, and forgiveness. If that sounds a lot like work, it is—which is perfectly fine with God. Why? Because He knows that you are capable of doing that work, and because He knows that the fruits of those labors will bring a rich harvest to you and to your loved ones.

## Great Ideas About...
# Love

Love wins when everything else will fail.

*Fanny Jackson Coppin*

He who is filled with love is filled with God Himself.

*St. Augustine*

Love stretches your heart and makes you big inside.

*Margaret Walker*

Carve your name on hearts, not on marble.

*C. H. Spurgeon*

There is always something left to love.
And if you haven't learned that,
you haven't learned nothing.

*Lorraine Hansberry*

*Love one another deeply, from the heart.*

*1 Peter 1:22 NIV*

*Above all, love each other deeply,*
*because love covers over a multitude of sins.*

*1 Peter 4:8 NIV*

## Today's Tip

The key to successful Christian living lies in your submission to the Spirit of God. If you call yourself a Christian, then God has commanded you to love people . . . and it's a commandment that covers both saints and sinners.

*Your Thoughts*

# HAPPINESS IS...

*A Result of Discipline*

*Therefore, get your minds ready for action,*
*being self-disciplined, and set your hope completely*
*on the grace to be brought to you*
*at the revelation of Jesus Christ.*

1 Peter 1:13 Holman CSB

Happiness is a way of life, a way of summoning the discipline that inevitably leads to success and accomplishment. So if you really want to be happy, you'll need to be a disciplined person, no exceptions.

God's Word reminds us again and again that our Creator expects us to lead disciplined lives. God doesn't reward laziness, misbehavior, or apathy. To the contrary, He expects believers to behave with dignity and discipline.

> *Apply your heart*
> *to discipline*
> *And your ears to*
> *words of knowledge.*
> *Proverbs 23:12 NASB*

We live in a world in which leisure is glorified and indifference is often glamorized. But God has other plans. He did not create us for lives of mediocrity; He created us for far greater things.

Life's greatest rewards seldom fall into our laps; to the contrary, our greatest accomplishments usually require lots of work, which is perfectly fine with God. After all, He knows that we're up to the task, and He has big plans for us. The rest, of course, is up to us.

## Great Ideas About ...
# Discipline

Self-discipline is an acquired asset.

*Duke Ellington*

As we seek to become disciples of Jesus Christ,
we should never forget that the word *disciple* is
directly related to the word *discipline*. To be a disciple of
the Lord Jesus Christ is to know his discipline.

*Dennis Swanberg*

Champions aren't made in gyms. Champions are made
from something they have deep inside them: a desire,
a dream, a vision. They have to have the skill and the will.
But the will must be stronger than the skill.

*Muhammad Ali*

Don't feel entitled to anything you didn't
sweat and struggle for.

*Marian Wright Edelman*

*God hasn't invited us into a disorderly, unkempt life*
*but into something holy and beautiful—*
*as beautiful on the inside as the outside.*

1 Thessalonians 4:7 MSG

*Discipline yourself for the purpose of godliness.*

1 Timothy 4:7 NASB

## Today's Tip

You need a library.  Pick and choose your books wisely.
Make sure they're going to build you up.
Be sure that your library makes you stronger,
healthier, and wiser.

*Your Thoughts*

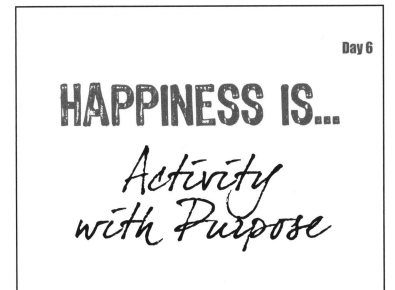

# HAPPINESS IS...

*Activity with Purpose*

May He give you what your heart desires
and fulfill your whole purpose.

*Psalm 20:4 Holman CSB*

Happiness is activity with purpose. And purpose, like everything else in the universe, begins in the heart of God. Whether you realize it or not, God has a direction for your life, a divine calling, a path along which He intends to lead you. When you welcome God into your heart and establish a genuine relationship with Him, He will begin—and He will continue—to make His purposes known.

Have you ever felt that you were just spinning your wheels? Just going through the motions? If so, you know that there's no fulfillment in purposeless living. Your job, therefore, is to keep searching for God's purpose in your life . . . and to keep searching until you find it.

> I urge you to live a life worthy of the calling you have received.
>
> *Ephesians 4:1 NIV*

Discovering God's unfolding purpose for your life is a daily journey, a journey guided by the teachings of God's Holy Word. As you reflect upon God's promises and upon the meaning that those promises hold for you, ask God to lead you throughout the coming day. Let your Heavenly Father direct your steps; concentrate on what God wants you to do now, and leave the distant future in hands that are far more capable than your own: His hands.

Sometimes, God's intentions will be clear to you; other times, God's plan will seem uncertain at best. But even on those difficult days when you are unsure which way to turn, you must never lose sight of these overriding facts: God created you for a reason; He has important work for you to do; and He's waiting patiently for you to do it. So why not begin today?

## Great Ideas About...
# Purpose

Many persons have a wrong idea of what constitutes
true happiness. It is not attained through self-gratification,
but through fidelity to a worthy purpose.

*Helen Keller*

Continually restate to yourself what the purpose of your life is.

*Oswald Chambers*

What we need are mental and spiritual giants
who are aflame with a purpose.

*Nannie Burroughs*

Without God, life has no purpose, and without purpose,
life has no meaning.

*Rick Warren*

Happiness is not a goal; it is a by-product.

*Eleanor Roosevelt*

*For it is God who is working among you both the willing*
*and the working for His good purpose.*

Philippians 2:13 Holman CSB

*We look at this Son and see the God who cannot be seen.*
*We look at this Son and see God's original purpose*
*in everything created.*

Colossians 1:15 MSG

## Today's Tip

Ten years from now you will be somewhere—the question is
where? You have the power to make that determination.
And remember: it's not about earning a living;
it's about designing a life.

*Your Thoughts*

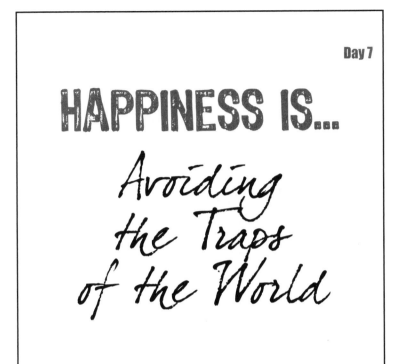

# HAPPINESS IS...

*Avoiding the Traps of the World*

*Do not love the world or the things that belong to the world.*
*If anyone loves the world, love for the Father is not in him.*

1 John 2:15 Holman CSB

Happiness Is . . .

All of mankind is engaged in a colossal, worldwide treasure hunt. Some folks seek treasure from earthly sources, treasures such as material wealth or public acclaim—these folks don't find enduring happiness because they're searching for it in the wrong places. Other people seek happiness by making God's promises the cornerstone of their lives—and these folks are blessed by the Creator.

What kind of treasure hunter are you? Are you so caught up in the demands of popular society that you sometimes allow the search for worldly treasures to become your primary focus? If so, it's time to reorganize your daily to-do list by placing God in His rightful place: first place.

> Set your minds on what is above, not on what is on the earth.
>
> *Colossians 3:2 Holman CSB*

If you sincerely seek to strengthen your character, you'll focus more intently on God's treasures and less intently on the world's treasures. Don't allow anyone or anything to separate you from your Heavenly Father and His only begotten Son.

Society's priorities are transitory; God's priorities are permanent. The world's treasures are difficult to find and difficult to keep; God's treasures are ever-present and everlasting. Which treasures and whose priorities will you claim as your own? The answer should be obvious.

36 —

# Great Ideas About...
# Worldliness

I'm fulfilled in what I do. I never thought that a lot of money or
fine clothes—the finer things of life—would make you happy.
My concept of happiness is to be filled in a spiritual sense.

*Coretta Scott King*

Too many Christians have geared their program to please,
to entertain, and to gain favor from this world.
We are concerned with how much, instead of how little,
like this age we can become.

*Billy Graham*

Aim at heaven and you will get earth thrown in;
aim at earth and you will get neither.

*C. S. Lewis*

The Doors of Wisdom are never shut.

*Ben Franklin*

Don't mistake pleasure for happiness.

*Josh Billings*

*For whatever is born of God overcomes the world.*
*And this is the victory that has overcome the world—our faith.*

1 John 5:4 NKJV

*Religion that God our Father accepts as pure and faultless is this:*
*to look after orphans and widows in their distress and to keep oneself*
*from being polluted by the world.*

James 1:27 NIV

## Today's Tip

If you dwell on the world's messages,
you're setting yourself up for disaster. If you dwell on
God's message, you're setting yourself up for victory.

*Your Thoughts*

# HAPPINESS IS...

*Sowing Generously*

Remember this: the person who sows sparingly
will also reap sparingly, and the person who
sows generously will also reap generously.

*2 Corinthians 9:6 Holman CSB*

I t's not too complicated: input determines output. What you sow is what you reap. If you want to be happy, sow generously; if not, sow sparsely.

The thread of generosity is woven—completely and inextricably—into the very fabric of Christ's teachings. As He sent His disciples out to heal the sick and spread God's message of salvation, Jesus offered this guiding principle: "Freely you have received, freely give" (Matthew 10:8 NIV). The principle still applies. If we are to be disciples of Christ, we must give freely of our time, our possessions, and our love.

In 2 Corinthians 9, Paul reminds us that when we sow the seeds of generosity, we reap bountiful rewards in accordance with God's plan for our lives. Thus, we are instructed to give cheerfully and without reservation: "But this I say, He which soweth sparingly shall reap also sparingly; and he which soweth bountifully shall reap also bountifully. Every man according as he purposeth in his heart, so let him give; not grudgingly, or of necessity: for God loveth a cheerful giver" (vv. 6-7 KJV). Today, make this pledge and keep it: Be a cheerful, generous, courageous giver. The world needs your help, and you need the spiritual rewards that will be yours when you give it.

> Be generous:
> Invest in acts of charity.
> Charity yields
> high returns.
>
> Ecclesiastes 11:1 MSG

## Great Ideas About...
# Generosity

Success has nothing to do with what you gain in life or
accomplish for yourself. It's what you do for others.

*Danny Thomas*


Find out how much God has given you and from it take what
you need; the remainder is needed by others.

*St. Augustine*


To show great love for God and our neighbor,
we need not do great things. It is how much love we put in
the doing that makes our offering something beautiful for God.

*Mother Teresa*


Service is the rent you pay for room on this earth.

*Shirley Chisholm*


The happiest people are those who do the most for others.

*Booker T. Washington*

*He did it with all his heart. So he prospered.*

2 Chronicles 31:21 NKJV

*Be strong and brave, and do the work.*
*Don't be afraid or discouraged, because the Lord God,*
*my God, is with you. He will not fail you or leave you.*

1 Chronicles 28:20 NCV

## Today's Tip

There is a direct relationship between generosity
and happiness—the more you give to others,
the more joy you will experience for yourself.

*Your Thoughts*

# HAPPINESS IS...

*Learning to Rejoice*

*Rejoice in the Lord always. Again I will say, rejoice!*

Philippians 4:4 NKJV

ve you made the choice to rejoice? If you're a Christian,
you have every reason to be joyful. After all, the ultimate
battle has already been won on the cross at Calvary. And
if your life has been transformed by Christ's sacrifice, then you, as
a recipient of God's grace, have every reason to live joyfully. Yet
sometimes, amid the inevitable hustle and bustle of life here on
earth, you may lose sight of your blessings as you wrestle with the
challenges of everyday life.

Do you seek happiness, abundance, and contentment? If
so, here are some things you should do: Love God and His Son;
depend upon God for strength; try, to the best of your abilities, to follow God's will; and strive to obey His Holy Word. When you do these things, you'll discover that happiness goes hand-in-hand with righteousness. The happiest people are not those
who rebel against God; the happiest people are those who love
God and obey His commandments.

> But let all who take
> refuge in You rejoice.
> *Psalm 5:11 Holman CSB*

What does life have in store for you? A world full of
possibilities (of course it's up to you to seize them) and God's
promise of abundance (of course it's up to you to accept it). So,
as you embark upon the next phase of your journey, remember to
celebrate the life that God has given you.

# Great Ideas About...
## Joy

If you can forgive the person you were, accept the person
you are, and believe in the person you will become,
you are headed for joy. So celebrate your life.

*Barbara Johnson*

The Christian lifestyle is not one of legalistic do's and don'ts,
but one that is positive, attractive, and joyful.

*Vonette Bright*

Joy is the direct result of having God's perspective on our daily
lives and the effect of loving our Lord enough to obey
His commands and trust His promises.

*Bill Bright*

Our sense of joy, satisfaction, and fulfillment in life increases,
no matter what the circumstances,
if we are in the center of God's will.

*Billy Graham*

Talk happiness. The world is sad enough without your woes.

*Ella Wheeler Wilcox*

*Rejoice, and be exceeding glad: for great is your reward in heaven . . . .*

*Matthew 5:12 KJV*

*I will thank you, LORD, with all my heart;*
*I will tell of all the marvelous things you have done.*
*I will be filled with joy because of you.*
*I will sing praises to your name, O Most High.*

*Psalm 9:1-2 NLT*

## Today's Tip

Joy does not depend upon your circumstances;
it depends upon your thoughts and upon
your relationship with God.

*Your Thoughts*

# HAPPINESS IS...

## Looking on the Sunny Side

*A cheerful heart has a continual feast.*

Proverbs 15:15 Holman CSB

Cheerfulness is a gift that we give to others and to ourselves. And, as believers who have been saved by a risen Christ, why shouldn't we be cheerful? The answer, of course, is that we have every reason to honor our Savior with joy in our hearts, smiles on our faces, and words of celebration on our lips.

How cheerful are you? Do you spend most of your day celebrating your life or complaining about it? If you're a big-time celebrator, keep celebrating. But if you've established the bad habit of looking at the hole instead of the donut, it's time to correct your spiritual vision.

> Be cheerful. Keep things in good repair. Keep your spirits up. Think in harmony. Be agreeable. Do all that, and the God of love and peace will be with you for sure.
>
> 2 Corinthians 13:11 MSG

Pessimism and doubt are two of the most important tools that the devil uses to achieve his objectives. Your challenge, of course, is to ensure that the devil cannot use these tools on you. So today, make sure to celebrate the life that God has given you. Your Creator has blessed you beyond measure. Honor Him with your prayers, your words, your deeds, and your joy.

## Great Ideas About...
# Cheerfulness

A cloudy day is no match for a sunny disposition.

*William Arthur Ward*

The people whom I have seen succeed best in life
have always been cheerful and hopeful people who went about
their business with a smile on their faces.

*Charles Kingsley*

God is good, and heaven is forever.
And if those two facts don't cheer you up, nothing will.

*Marie T. Freeman*

We may run, walk, stumble, drive, or fly,
but let us never lose sight of the reason for the journey,
or miss a chance to see a rainbow on the way.

*Gloria Gaither*

Christ can put a spring in your step and a thrill in your heart.
Optimism and cheerfulness are products of knowing Christ.

*Billy Graham*

*Do everything readily and cheerfully—no bickering,
no second-guessing allowed! Go out into the world uncorrupted,
a breath of fresh air in this squalid and polluted society.
Provide people with a glimpse of good living and of the living God.
Carry the light-giving Message into the night.*

*Philippians 2:14-15 MSG*

## Today's Tip

Do you need a little cheering up?
Cheer up somebody else. When you brighten somebody else's
day, you brighten up your own day, too.

*Your Thoughts*

# HAPPINESS IS...

## Living in Accordance with Your Beliefs

*Do what God's teaching says;*
*when you only listen and do nothing,*
*you are fooling yourselves.*

James 1:22 NCV

Life is a series of choices. Each day, we make countless decisions that can bring us closer to God . . . or not. When we live according to God's commandments, we earn for ourselves the abundance and peace that He intends for our lives. But, when we turn our backs upon God by ignoring Him—or by disobeying Him—we bring needless pain and suffering upon ourselves and our families.

> Don't be deceived:
> God is not mocked.
> For whatever a man
> sows he will also reap,
> because the one who
> sows to his flesh will
> reap corruption from
> the flesh, but the one who
> sows to the Spirit will
> reap eternal life from
> the Spirit.
>
> Galatians 6:7-8 Holman CSB

Do you want God's peace and His blessings? Then obey Him. When you're faced with a difficult choice or a powerful temptation, seek God's counsel and trust the counsel He gives. Invite God into your heart and live according to His commandments. And when God speaks to you through that little quiet voice that He has placed in your heart, listen. When you do, you will be blessed today, and tomorrow, and forever. And you'll discover that happiness means living in accordance with your beliefs. No exceptions.

## Great Ideas About...
# Behavior

The time is always right to do what is right.

*Martin Luther King, Jr.*

If you want to be respected for your actions,
then your behavior must be above reproach.

*Rosa Parks*

Don't worry about what you do not understand.
Worry about what you do understand in the Bible
but do not live by.

*Corrie ten Boom*

When you discover the Christian way,
you discover your own way as a person.

*E. Stanley Jones*

Christianity says we were created by a righteous God to flourish
and be exhilarated in a righteous environment.
God has "wired" us in such a way that the more righteous
we are, the more we'll actually enjoy life.

*Bill Hybels*

*Therefore, get your minds ready for action, being self-disciplined, and set your hope completely on the grace to be brought to you at the revelation of Jesus Christ. As obedient children, do not be conformed to the desires of your former ignorance but, as the One who called you is holy, you also are to be holy in all your conduct.*

1 Peter 1:13-15 Holman CSB

## Today's Tip

Face it: talking about your beliefs is easy. But, making your actions match your words is much harder! Why? Because you are a normal human being, and that means that you can be tempted by stuff and by people. Nevertheless, if you really want to be honest with yourself, then you must make your actions match your beliefs. Period.

*Your Thoughts*

# HAPPINESS IS...

*Freedom from Fear*

*Do not be afraid or discouraged.*
*For the LORD your God is with you wherever you go.*

Joshua 1:9 NLT

Happiness is freedom from fear—but sometimes, it's hard to live courageously. Why? Because we live in a fear-based world, a world where bad news travels at light speed and good news doesn't. These are troubled times, times when we have legitimate fears for the future of our nation, our world, and our families. But as Christians, we have every reason to live courageously. After all, the ultimate battle has already been fought and won on that faraway cross at Calvary.

> But when Jesus heard it, He answered him, "Don't be afraid. Only believe."
>
> Luke 8:50 Holman CSB

Perhaps you, like countless other believers, have found your courage tested by the anxieties and fears that are an inevitable part of 21st-century life. If so, God wants to have a little talk with you. The next time you find your courage tested to the limit, God wants to remind you that He is not just near; He is here.

Your Heavenly Father is your Protector and your Deliverer. Call upon Him whenever you need Him . . . and be comforted. Whatever your challenge, whatever your trouble, God can handle it. And will.

## Great Ideas About ...
# Courage

God did away with all my fear.

*Rosa Parks*

There comes a time when we simply have to face
the challenges in our lives and stop backing down.

*John Eldredge*

Just as courage is faith in good, so discouragement
is faith in evil, and while courage opens the door to good,
discouragement opens it to evil.

*Hannah Whitall Smith*

Fear brings out the worst in everybody.

*Maya Angelou*

I have a lot of things to prove to myself.
One is that I can live my life fearlessly.

*Oprah Winfrey*

*But He said to them, "Why are you fearful, you of little faith?"*
*Then He got up and rebuked the winds and the sea.*
*And there was a great calm.*

Matthew 8:26 Holman CSB

### Today's Tip

Are you feeling anxious or fearful?
If so, trust God to handle those problems that are simply
too big for you to solve. Entrust the future—and your future—
to God. Then, spend a few minutes thinking about specific steps
you can take to confront—and conquer—your fears.

*Your Thoughts*

---

---

---

---

---

---

---

---

# HAPPINESS IS...

*Learning to Forgive Others (and Yourself)*

*All bitterness, anger and wrath, insult and slander must be removed from you, along with all wickedness. And be kind and compassionate to one another, forgiving one another, just as God also forgave you in Christ.*

*Ephesians 4:31-32 Holman CSB*

It's a fact: if you can't forgive, you're not free . . . and you're not happy.

Are you mired in the quicksand of bitterness or regret? If so, you are not only disobeying God's Word, you are also wasting your time.

> Whenever you stand praying, forgive, if you have anything against anyone, so that your Father in heaven will also forgive you your transgressions.
>
> Mark 11:25 NASB

Being imperfect human beings, most of us are quick to anger, quick to blame, slow to forgive, and even slower to forget. Yet as Christians, we are commanded to forgive others, just as we, too, have been forgiven.

If there exists even one person—alive or dead—against whom you hold bitter feelings, it's time to forgive. Or, if you are angry with yourself for some past mistake or shortcoming, it's finally time to forgive yourself and move on. Hatred, bitterness, and regret are not part of God's plan for your life. Forgiveness is.

## Great Ideas About...
# Forgiveness

Learning how to forgive and forget
is one of the secrets of a happy Christian life.

*Warren Wiersbe*

Forgiveness is nothing compared to forgetting.

*Bessie Delaney*

Our relationships with other people are of primary importance
to God. Because God is love, He cannot tolerate
any unforgiveness or hardness in us toward any individual.

*Catherine Marshall*

Forgiveness is not an emotion.
Forgiveness is an act of the will, and the will can
function regardless of the temperature of the heart.

*Corrie ten Boom*

Develop and maintain the capacity to forgive.

*Martin Luther King, Jr.*

*Be even-tempered, content with second place, quick to forgive an offense. Forgive as quickly and completely as the Master forgave you. And regardless of what else you put on, wear love. It's your basic, all-purpose garment. Never be without it.*

Colossians 3:13-14 MSG

## Today's Tip

What if it's really hard to forgive somebody? If forgiveness were easy, everybody would be doing it—but it's not always easy to forgive and forget. If you simply can't seem to forgive somebody, pray about it . . . and keep praying about it . . . until God helps you do the right thing.

*Your Thoughts*

# HAPPINESS IS...

*Having Happy Friends*

A friend loves you all the time,
and a brother helps in time of trouble.
*Proverbs 17:17 NCV*

D o you want to be happy? Then make sure that you pick out friends who are happy, too. Why? Because happiness, like all human emotions, is contagious.

When you associate with positive people, you'll feel better about yourself and your world—but when you hang around with negative people, you won't. So if you really want to feel better about yourself and your circumstances, you'll need to think carefully about the friends you choose to make—and the ones you choose to keep.

> As iron sharpens iron, so people can improve each other.
>
> Proverbs 27:17 NCV

If you're really serious about being an optimistic, upbeat, hope-filled person, make sure that your friends feel the same way. Because if you become involved with upbeat people, you'll tend to be an upbeat person, too. But if you hang out with the critics, the cynics, and the naysayers, you'll find yourself becoming a cynic, too. And life is far too short for that.

## Great Ideas About...
# Friendship

A friend is a present you give yourself.

*Robert Louis Stevenson*

The glory of friendship is not the outstretched hand,
or the kindly smile, or the joy of companionship.
It is the spiritual inspiration that comes to one when
he discovers that someone else believes in him
and is willing to trust him with his friendship.

*Corrie ten Boom*

In friendship, God opens your eyes to the glories of Himself.

*Joni Eareckson Tada*

A friend gathers all the pieces and gives them back
in the right order.

*Toni Morrison*

To get the full value of joy, you have to have someone
to divide it with.

*Mark Twain*

*Beloved, if God so loved us, we also ought to love one another.*

*1 John 4:11 NKJV*

*This is my command: Love one another the way I loved you.*
*This is the very best way to love.*
*Put your life on the line for your friends.*

*John 15:12-13 MSG*

## Today's Tip

Your friends will have a major impact on your self-image.
That's an important reason (but not the only reason)
to select your friends carefully.

*Your Thoughts*

_____

_____

_____

_____

_____

_____

_____

_____

_____

# HAPPINESS IS...

## A Thankful Heart

*Enter into His gates with thanksgiving,*
*and into His courts with praise. Be thankful to Him,*
*and bless His name. For the LORD is good;*
*His mercy is everlasting, and His truth*
*endures to all generations.*

Psalm 100:4-5 NKJV

Thankful people are happy people. Are you a thankful person? Do you appreciate the gifts that God has given you? And, do you demonstrate your gratitude by being a faithful steward of the gifts and talents that you have received from your Creator? You most certainly should be thankful. After all, when you stop to think about it, God has given you more blessings than you can count. So the question of the day is this: will you thank your Heavenly Father . . . or will you spend your time and energy doing other things?

> *In everything give thanks; for this is the will of God in Christ Jesus for you.*
>
> *1 Thessalonians 5:18 NKJV*

The coming day is a canvas upon which you can compose a beautiful work of art if you choose to do so. So today, look for good things to do and good things to be thankful for. If you look carefully, you won't need to look very far. And remember: when it comes time to count your blessings, nobody can count them for you.

God is always listening—are you willing to say thanks? It's up to you, and the next move is always yours.

## Great Ideas About...
# Thanksgiving

Any day you wake up is a good day.

*Duke Ellington*

No duty is more urgent than that of returning thanks.

*St. Ambrose*

Thanksgiving or complaining—these words express
two contrastive attitudes of the souls of God's children
in regard to His dealings with them. The soul that gives thanks
can find comfort in everything; the soul that complains
can find comfort in nothing.

*Hannah Whitall Smith*

When it comes to life, the critical thing is whether you
take things for granted or take them with gratitude.

*G. K. Chesterton*

God gave you a gift of 86,400 seconds today.
Have you used one to say thank you?

*William Arthur Ward*

*Thanks be to God for His indescribable gift.*

2 Corinthians 9:15 Holman CSB

*It is good to give thanks to the LORD,*
*And to sing praises to Your name, O Most High.*

Psalm 92:1 NKJV

## Today's Tip

God gives each of us more blessings than we can count.
Those blessings include life, family, freedom, friends, talents,
and possessions, just for starters. Winners recognize the size
and scope of God's blessings—and real winners (like you)
spend plenty of time thanking Him.

*Your Thoughts*

_____

_____

_____

_____

_____

_____

_____

_____

# HAPPINESS IS...

## Learning How to Endure Hardships with Patience and Trust

*Consider it pure joy, my brothers, whenever you face trials of many kinds, because you know that the testing of your faith develops perseverance. Perseverance must finish its work so that you may be mature and complete, not lacking anything.*

James 1:2-4 NIV

Happiness is learning how to deal with the inevitable disappointments of life. When we are troubled, God stands ready and willing to protect us. Our responsibility, of course, is to ask Him for protection. When we call upon Him in heartfelt prayer, He will answer—in His own time and in accordance with His own perfect plan.

> We are pressured
> in every way
> but not crushed;
> we are perplexed
> but not in despair.
>
> 2 Corinthians 4:8 Holman CSB

Life is often challenging, but we must not be afraid. God loves us, and He will protect us. In times of hardship, He will comfort us; in times of sorrow, He will dry our tears. When we are troubled or weak or sorrowful, God is always with us. We must build our lives on the rock that cannot be shaken: we must trust in God. And then, we must get on with the hard work of tackling our problems . . . because if we don't, who will? Or should?

## Great Ideas About...
# Adversity

Never let your head hang down. Never give up and sit down
and grieve. Find another way.

*Satchel Paige*

Recently I've been learning that life comes down to this:
God is in everything. Regardless of what difficulties
I am experiencing at the moment, or what things aren't as
I would like them to be, I look at the circumstances and say,
"Lord, what are you trying to teach me?"

*Catherine Marshall*

The ultimate measure of a man is not where he stands
in moments of comfort, but where he stands
at times of challenge and controversy.

*Martin Luther King, Jr.*

The size of your burden is never as important
as the way you carry it.

*Lena Horne*

*We also have joy with our troubles,
because we know that these troubles produce patience.
And patience produces character, and character produces hope.*

Romans 5:3-4 NCV

*The LORD lifts the burdens of those bent beneath their loads.
The LORD loves the righteous.*

Psalm 146:8 NLT

## Today's Tip

When tough times arrive, you should work as if everything
depends on you and pray as if everything depends on God.

*Your Thoughts*

_____

_____

_____

_____

_____

_____

_____

_____

# HAPPINESS IS...

## Learning Not to Judge Others

*Do not judge, and you will not be judged.*
*Do not condemn, and you will not be condemned.*
*Forgive, and you will be forgiven.*

Luke 6:37 Holman CSB

Would you like a surefire formula for being unhappy? Here it is: spend as much time as you can judging other people. But if you'd rather be happy, please remember this: in matters of judgment, God does not need (or want) your help. Why? Because God is perfectly capable of judging the human heart . . . while you are not. This message was made clear by the teachings of Jesus.

As Jesus came upon a young woman who had been condemned by the Pharisees, He spoke not only to the crowd that was gathered there, but also to all generations, when He warned, "He that is without sin among you, let him first cast a stone at her" (John 8:7 KJV).

Christ's message is straightforward: because we are all sinners, we are commanded to refrain from judging others. Yet, the irony is this: it is precisely because we are sinners that we are so quick to judge.

> *You, therefore, have no excuse, you who pass judgment on someone else, for at whatever point you judge the other, you are condemning yourself.*
>
> Romans 2:1 NIV

All of us have fallen short of God's laws, and none of us, therefore, is qualified to "cast the first stone." Thankfully, God has forgiven us, and we, too, must forgive others. Let us refrain, then, from judging our family members, our friends, and our loved ones. Instead, let us forgive them and love them in the same way that God has forgiven us.

## Great Ideas About...
# Judging Others

God is the only judge. You are just his emissary of peace.

*St. Thérèse of Lisieux*

Being critical of others, including God,
is one way we try to avoid facing and judging our own sins.

*Warren Wiersbe*

Turn your attention upon yourself and beware of judging
the deeds of other men, for in judging others a man labors
vainly, often makes mistakes, and easily sins; whereas,
in judging and taking stock of himself he does something
that is always profitable.

*Thomas à Kempis*

Christians think they are prosecuting attorneys or judges,
when, in reality, God has called all of us to be witnesses.

*Warren Wiersbe*

Don't judge other people more harshly
than you want God to judge you.

*Marie T. Freeman*

*Why do you look at the speck of sawdust in your brother's eye and pay no attention to the plank in your own eye? How can you say to your brother, "Let me take the speck out of your eye," when all the time there is a plank in your own eye? You hypocrite, first take the plank out of your own eye, and then you will see clearly to remove the speck from your brother's eye.*

*Matthew 7:3-5 NIV*

## Today's Tip

Your ability to judge others requires
a divine insight that you simply don't have.
So do everybody (including yourself) a favor: don't judge.

*Your Thoughts*

_____

_____

_____

_____

_____

_____

_____

_____

# HAPPINESS IS...

## *Counting Your Blessings*

*For surely, O LORD, you bless the righteous;*
*you surround them with your favor as with a shield.*

*Psalm 5:12 NIV*

I f you sat down and began counting your blessings, how long would it take? A very, very long time! Your blessings include life, freedom, family, friends, talents, and possessions, for starters. But, your greatest blessing—a gift that is yours for the asking—is God's gift of salvation through Christ Jesus.

Are you a thankful believer who takes time each day to take a partial inventory of the gifts that God has given you? Hopefully you are that kind of Christian. After all, God's Word makes it clear: a happy heart is a thankful heart.

> Blessings crown the head
> of the righteous . . . .
> Proverbs 10:6 NIV

We honor God, in part, by the genuine gratitude we feel in our hearts for the blessings He has bestowed upon us. Yet even the most saintly among us must endure periods of fear, doubt, and regret. Why? Because we are imperfect human beings who are incapable of perfect gratitude. Still, even on life's darker days, we must seek to cleanse our hearts of negative emotions and fill them, instead, with praise, with love, with hope, and with thanksgiving. To do otherwise is to be unfair to ourselves, to our loved ones, and to our God.

Today, begin making a list of your blessings. You most certainly will not be able to make a complete list, but take a few moments and jot down as many blessings as you can. Then, give thanks to the Giver of all good things: God. His love for you is eternal, as are His gifts. And it's never too soon—or too late—to offer Him thanks.

## Great Ideas About...
# Blessings

Blessings we enjoy daily; and for the most of them, because
they are so common, most men forget to pay their praise.

*Izaak Walton*

There is no secret that can separate you from God's love;
there is no secret that can separate you from His blessings;
there is no secret that is worth keeping from His grace.

*Serita Ann Jakes*

God is more anxious to bestow His blessings on us
than we are to receive them.

*St. Augustine*

God blesses us in spite of our lives and not because of our lives.

*Max Lucado*

Think of the blessings we so easily take for granted: Life itself;
preservation from danger; every bit of health we enjoy;
every hour of liberty; the ability to see, to hear, to speak,
to think, and to imagine all this comes from the hand of God.

*Billy Graham*

*The LORD is kind and merciful, slow to get angry,
full of unfailing love. The LORD is good to everyone.
He showers compassion on all his creation.*

Psalm 145:8-9 NLT

*The LORD bless you and keep you;
The LORD make His face shine upon you,
And be gracious to you.*

Numbers 6:24-25 NKJV

## Today's Tip

Carve out time to thank God for His blessings.
Take time out of every day (not just on Sundays)
to praise God and thank Him for His gifts.

*Your Thoughts*

# HAPPINESS IS...

## Learning to Worry Less and Trust God More

Give all your worries and cares to God,
for he cares about what happens to you.

*1 Peter 5:6 NLT*

Have you acquired the habit of worrying about almost everything under the sun? If so, it's a habit you should break. Why? Because happiness and worry can't live together in the same human heart—they are emotions which are mutually exclusive. So if you want to be happier (not to mention healthier), you must find ways to worry less. But "worrying less" isn't always easy.

Even if you're a very faithful Christian, you may be plagued by occasional periods of discouragement and doubt. Even though you trust God's promise of salvation—even though you sincerely believe in God's love and protection—you may find yourself upset by the countless details of everyday life. Jesus understood your concerns when He spoke the reassuring words found in the 6th chapter of Matthew:

"Therefore I say to you, do not worry about your life, what you will eat or what you will drink; nor about your body, what you will put on. Is not life more than food and the body more than clothing? Look at the birds of the air, for they neither sow nor reap nor gather into barns; yet your heavenly Father feeds them. Are you not of more value than they? Which of you by worrying can add one cubit to his stature? . . . Therefore do not worry about tomorrow, for tomorrow will worry about its own things. Sufficient for the day is its own trouble. " (vv. 25-27, 34 NKJV)

> *What time I am afraid,*
> *I will trust in thee.*
> Psalm 56:3 KJV

Where is the best place to take your worries? Take them to God. Take your troubles to Him; take your fears to Him; take your doubts to Him; take your weaknesses to Him; take your sorrows to Him . . . and leave them all there. Seek protection from the One who offers you eternal salvation; build your spiritual house upon the Rock that cannot be moved.

Perhaps you are concerned about your future, your relationships, or your finances. Or perhaps you are simply a "worrier" by nature. If so, choose to make Matthew 6 a regular part of your daily Bible reading. This beautiful passage will remind you that God still sits in His heaven and you are His beloved child. Then, perhaps, you will worry a little less and trust God a little more, and that's as it should be because God is trustworthy . . . and you are protected.

## Great Ideas About...
# Trusting God

Remember always that there are two things which are more
utterly incompatible even than oil and water,
and these two are trust and worry.

*Hannah Whitall Smith*

There are two kinds of worries—those you can do something
about and those you can't. Don't spend any time on the latter.

*Duke Ellington*

Worry is simply thinking the same thing over and over again . . .
and not doing anything about it.

*Branch Rickey*

*Do not worry about anything, but pray and ask God*
*for everything you need, always giving thanks.*

*Philippians 4:6 NCV*

*Give your worries to the Lord, and he will take care of you.*
*He will never let good people down.*

*Psalm 55:22 NCV*

## Today's Tip

Focus on your work, not your worries:
Worry is never a valid substitute for work. So get out there,
do your best, and leave the rest up to God.

*Your Thoughts*

_____

_____

_____

_____

_____

_____

_____

_____

# HAPPINESS IS...

## Accepting God's Abundance

*I have come that they may have life,*
*and that they may have it more abundantly.*

John 10:10 NKJV

God offers us abundance, but He doesn't force it upon us. He promises that we "might have life" and that we "might have it more abundantly." And how, precisely can we claim that abundance? By obeying God and following His Son, that's how!

When we commit our hearts, our days, and our work to the One who created us, we experience spiritual abundance. But, when we focus our thoughts and energies, not upon God's will for our lives, but instead upon our own unending assortments of earthly needs and desires, we inevitably forfeit the spiritual abundance that might otherwise be ours.

> These things have
> I spoken unto you,
> that my joy might
> remain in you, and that
> your joy might be full.
>
> John 15:11 KJV

Today and every day, seek God's will for your life and follow it. Today, turn your worries and your concerns over to your Heavenly Father. Today, seek God's wisdom, follow His commandments, trust His judgment, and honor His Son. And while you're at it, get rid of that critical voice inside your head—the little voice that tells you you're never quite good enough. When you do these things, you'll receive God's abundance . . . and you'll be happy.

## Great Ideas About...
# Abundance

God loves you and wants you to experience peace
and life—abundant and eternal.

*Billy Graham*


We honor God by asking for great things when they are a part of
His promise. We dishonor Him and cheat ourselves when
we ask for molehills where He has promised mountains.

*Vance Havner*


Greatness occurs when your children love you, when your critics
respect you, and when you have peace of mind.

*Quincy Jones*


God is the giver, and we are the receivers. And His richest gifts
are bestowed not upon those who do the greatest things,
but upon those who accept His abundance and His grace.

*Hannah Whitall Smith*


You can have it all; you just can't have it all at once.

*Oprah Winfrey*

*And God will generously provide all you need. Then you will always
have everything you need and plenty left over to share with others.*

*2 Corinthians 9:8 NLT*

*Ask and it will be given to you; seek and you will find;
knock and the door will be opened to you.
For everyone who asks receives; he who seeks finds;
and to him who knocks, the door will be opened.*

*Matthew 7:7-8 NIV*

## Today's Tip

Abundance and obedience go hand-in-hand.
Obey God first and expect to receive
His abundance second, not vice versa.

*Your Thoughts*

# HAPPINESS IS...

## Using Your Talents

The man who had received the five talents brought the other five. "Master," he said, "you entrusted me with five talents. See, I have gained five more." His master replied, "Well done, good and faithful servant! You have been faithful with a few things; I will put you in charge of many things. Come and share your master's happiness."

*Matthew 25:20-21 NIV*

If you squander your talents, you'll never really be happy. So here's a question for you: are you really using the talents that God has given you, or are you just coasting through life?

God knew precisely what He was doing when He gave you a unique set of talents and opportunities. And now, your Heavenly Father wants you to be a faithful steward of the gifts He has given you. But you live in a society that may encourage you to do otherwise. You face countless temptations to squander your time, your resources, and your talents. So you must be keenly aware of the inevitable distractions that can waste your energy, your time, your talents, and your opportunities.

> Now there are varieties of gifts, but the same Spirit. And there are varieties of ministries, and the same Lord.
>
> 1 Corinthians 12:4-5 NASB

Every day of your life, you have a choice to make: to nurture your talents or neglect them. When you choose wisely, God rewards your efforts, and He expands your opportunities to serve Him.

God has blessed you with unique opportunities to serve Him, and He has given you every tool that you need to do so. Today, accept this challenge: value the talent that God has given you, nourish it, make it grow, and share it with the world. After all, the best way to say "Thank You" for God's gifts is to use them.

## Great Ideas About ...
# Talents

Just don't give up trying to do what you really want to do.
Where there's love and inspiration,
I don't think you can go wrong.

*Ella Fitzgerald*


In the long run, it makes little difference how cleverly others are
deceived; if we are not doing what we are best equipped to do,
there will be a core of unhappiness in our lives which will
be more and more difficult to ignore as the years pass.

*Dorothea Brande*


Happiness lies in the joy of achievement
and the thrill of creative effort.

*Franklin D. Roosevelt*


Everyone has a talent for something.

*Marian Anderson*


The secret of a happy life is to do your duty and trust in God.

*Sam Jones*

*Do not neglect the gift that is in you.*

*1 Timothy 4:14 Holman CSB*

*I remind you to keep ablaze the gift of God that is in you.*

*2 Timothy 1:6 Holman CSB*

## Today's Tip

You are the sole owner of your own set of talents and opportunities. God has given you your own particular gifts—the rest is up to you.

*Your Thoughts*

# HAPPINESS IS...

## Learning to Control Negative Emotions

*My dear brothers and sisters, always be willing to listen and slow to speak. Do not become angry easily, because anger will not help you live the right kind of life God wants.*

James 1:19-20 NCV

Happiness is freedom from all those pesky negative emotions: emotions such as worry, low self-esteem, envy, greed, resentment, prejudice, hatred, and discouragement, for starters. Of course, the list of self-defeating emotions doesn't stop there, but you get the idea.

So what can you do to deliver yourself from the evils of these misdirected thoughts? Well, you can start by slowing down, stepping back, and thinking carefully about the things you've been thinking . . . and why. And while you're thinking things through, you'll want to recount your blessings, "re-thank" your Creator, and review who—or what—may be pulling your emotional strings.

Human emotions are highly variable, decidedly unpredictable, and often unreliable. Our emotions are like the weather, only sometimes far more fickle. So we must learn to reign in the negative thoughts that might otherwise derail our days and our lives. In short, we must learn to reject negative emotions and the negative people who spread them around.

> *The heart knows its own bitterness, and a stranger does not share its joy.*
>
> Proverbs 14:10 NKJV

Some folks are just plain gloomy . . . about everything. These unfortunate people have nothing good to say about anybody, and they'll encourage you to join in their misery. You can choose to join in if you want, but you're better off if you don't. In fact, if you want to remain healthy and happy, you'll work hard to steer clear of these negativity specialists.

Who's pulling your emotional strings? Are you allowing highly emotional people or highly-charged situations to dictate your moods, or are you wiser than that?

Sometime during the coming days, you may encounter a tough situation or a difficult person. And as a result, you may be gripped by a strong negative emotion. Distrust it. Reign it in. Test it. And turn it over to God.

Your emotions will inevitably change; God will not. So trust Him completely. When you do, you'll be surprised at how quickly those negative feelings can evaporate into thin air.

## Great Ideas About...
# Bitterness

We plant seeds that will flower as results in our lives,
so best to remove the weeds of anger, avarice, envy and doubt,
that peace and abundance may manifest for all.

*Dorothy Day*

When we get rid of inner conflicts and wrong attitudes
toward life, we will almost automatically burst into joy.

*E. Stanley Jones*

Don't bring negatives to my door.

*Maya Angelou*

*Do not be afraid or discouraged,*
*for the LORD is the one who goes before you.*
*He will be with you; he will neither fail you nor forsake you.*

Deuteronomy 31:8 NLT

*But as for you, be strong; don't be discouraged,*
*for your work has a reward.*

2 Chronicles 15:7 Holman CSB

## Today's Tip

Negative thinking breeds more negative thinking,
so nip negativity in the bud, starting today
and continuing every day of your life.

*Your Thoughts*

# HAPPINESS IS...

## Learning to Accept the Past

One thing I do, forgetting those things which are behind
and reaching forward to those things which are ahead,
I press toward the goal for the prize of the upward call
of God in Christ Jesus.

*Philippians 3:13-14 NKJV*

You'll never find lasting happiness unless you learn to make peace with the past. You'll never be contented until you learn how to look back upon your own experiences—both your victories and your disappointments—with a sense of acceptance and thanksgiving. In short, you must learn how to interpret your own personal history in a positive way.

Have you made peace with your past? If so, congratulations. But, if you're still mired in the quicksand of regret, it's time to plan your escape. How can you do so? By accepting what has been and by trusting God for what will be.

> Give in to God, come to terms with him and everything will turn out just fine.
>
> Job 22:21 MSG

Because you're only human, you may be slow to forget yesterday's setbacks; if so you are not alone. But if you sincerely want to find enduring happiness, you must find ways to entrust the past to God and then move on with your life.

If you have not yet made peace with the past, this is the day to declare an end to all hostilities. When you do, you can then direct your thoughts to the exciting future that God has in store for you.

## Great Ideas About...
# Acceptance

Have courage for the great sorrows of life and patience for
the small ones, and when you have laboriously accomplished
your daily task, go to sleep in peace. God is awake.

*Victor Hugo*


We must meet our disappointments, our persecutions,
our malicious enemies, our provoking friends, our trials and
temptations of every sort, with an attitude of surrender and trust.
We must spread our wings and "mount up" to the
"heavenly places in Christ."

*Hannah Whitall Smith*


Surrender to the Lord is not a tremendous sacrifice,
not an agonizing performance.
It is the most sensible thing you can do.

*Corrie ten Boom*


We must accept finite disappointment,
but we must never lose infinite hope.

*Martin Luther King, Jr.*

*Do not remember the past events, pay no attention to things of old.*
*Look, I am about to do something new; even now it is coming.*
*Do you not see it? Indeed, I will make a way in the wilderness,*
*rivers in the desert.*

*Isaiah 43:18-19 Holman CSB*

## Today's Tip

Maybe you think your past has been negative.
But God doesn't build anything on a negative.
He always builds on a positive.  So don't focus on
the negatives in your past . . . focus on the positives.

*Your Thoughts*

# HAPPINESS IS...

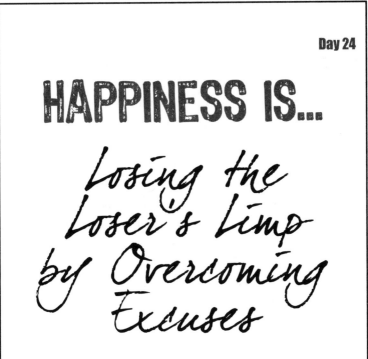

*Losing the Loser's Limp by Overcoming Excuses*

Don't be fooled by those who try to excuse these sins,
for the terrible anger of God comes upon
all those who disobey him.

*Ephesians 5:6 NLT*

appiness is growing up. And you will never grow up—you will never mature into a fully functioning adult—until you're willing to accept responsibility for your thoughts, your motives, your words, and your actions. You must toss away all the excuses for failure, and you must stop playing the blame game. In other words, you must rid yourself of the "loser's limp"—blaming your poor performance on imagined injuries—and you must face up to your mistakes.

All too often we're encouraged to proclaim ourselves "victims;" it's a handy way to avoid taking responsibility for our actions. So we make excuses, excuses, and more excuses—with predictably poor results.

> *Make your own attitude that of Christ Jesus.*
>
> Philippians 2:5 Holman CSB

We live in a world where excuses are everywhere. And it's precisely because excuses are so numerous that they are also so ineffective. When we hear the words, "I'm sorry but . . . ," most of us already know exactly what is to follow—the big excuse. The dog ate the homework. Traffic was terrible. It's the company's fault. The boss is to blame. The equipment is broken. We're out of that. And so forth, and so on.

Because we humans are such creative excuse-makers, all of the really good excuses have already been taken. In fact, the high-quality excuses have been used, re-used, over-used, and abused. That's why excuses don't work—we've heard them all before.

So, if you're wasting your time trying to portray yourself as a victim, or if you're trying to concoct a new and improved excuse, don't bother. Excuses don't work, and while you're inventing them, neither do you. So get rid of the loser's limp. Today.

## Great Ideas About...
## Excuses

One thing I don't believe in: excuses.

*Karl Malone*

Hold yourself responsible for a higher standard than anybody
expects of you. Never excuse yourself. Never pity yourself.
Be a hard master to yourself and be lenient to everybody else.

*Henry Ward Beecher*

Replace your excuses with fresh determination.

*Charles Swindoll*

Making up a string of excuses is usually
harder than doing the work.

*Marie T. Freeman*

*Do not lack diligence; be fervent in spirit; serve the Lord.*

Romans 12:11 Holman CSB

*Observe people who are good at their work—*
*skilled workers are always in demand and admired;*
*they don't take a back seat to anyone.*

Proverbs 22:29 MSG

## Today's Tip

Today, think of something important that you've been putting off. Then think of the excuses you've used to avoid that responsibility. Finally, ask yourself what you can do today to finish the work you've been avoiding.

*Your Thoughts*

# HAPPINESS IS...

## *Listening to Your Conscience*

*Now the goal of our instruction is love from a pure heart, a good conscience, and a sincere faith.*

1 Timothy 1:5 Holman CSB

o you want to be happy? Then you must live in accordance with your beliefs. Why? Because if you believe one thing but do something else, your conscience simply won't allow you to enjoy the peace and contentment that can—and should—be yours.

God gave you a conscience for a very good reason: to use it. But, as Billy Graham correctly observed, "Most of us follow our conscience as we follow a wheelbarrow. We push it in front of us in the direction we want to go." To do so, of course, is a very big mistake. Yet all of us, on occasion, have failed to listen to the voice that God planted in our hearts, and all of us have suffered the consequences.

> I will maintain my righteousness and never let go of it; my conscience will not reproach me as long as I live.
>
> Job 27:6 NIV

Is your life a picture book of your creed? Are your actions consistent with your personal code? And are you willing to practice the philosophy that you preach? If so, you're both wise and blessed. But if you're doing things that don't meet with approval of the person you see in the mirror, it's time to slow down, to step back, and to think about how your conduct is shaping your character. If you profess to be a Christian but behave yourself as if you were not, you're living in denial, which, by the way, is a very unhappy place to live.

So today, make certain that your actions are guided by God's Word and by the conscience that He has placed in your heart.

Don't treat your faith as if it were separate from everyday life—instead, weave your beliefs into the very fabric of your day. When you do, God will honor your good works, your good works will honor God, and everybody will be happy.

## Great Ideas About...
# Conscience

Reason often makes mistakes, but conscience never does.

*Josh Billings*

Your conscience is your alarm system. It's your protection.

*Charles Stanley*

It is neither safe nor prudent to do anything
against one's conscience.

*Martin Luther*

God desires that we become spiritually healthy enough
through faith to have a conscience that rightly interprets
the work of the Holy Spirit.

*Beth Moore*

*Blessed are those who have a tender conscience,*
*but the stubborn are headed for serious trouble.*

*Proverbs 28:14 NLT*

*Behold, the kingdom of God is within you.*

*Luke 17:21 KJV*

## Today's Tip

The more important the decision . . . the more carefully you
should listen to your conscience.

*Your Thoughts*

---

# HAPPINESS IS...

## A Choice

*I am not telling you this because I need anything.*
*I have learned to be satisfied with the things I have*
*and with everything that happens. I know how to live when*
*I am poor, and I know how to live when I have plenty.*
*I have learned the secret of being happy*
*at any time in everything that happens.*

*Philippians 4:11-12 NCV*

Happiness is a choice—it depends on how you interpret life. To be happy, you must learn to interpret the world and its events in a positive fashion. This means that you begin programming yourself to see the good in everything—no matter what happens, no matter what goes down. Then, when you find the good in every situation, you take that good, and you build upon it.

It's amazing how many people, especially those who portray themselves as "victims," conclude that the lives they're experiencing have been chosen for them. But they're mistaken. In truth, their lives—all of our lives—are composed of our choices . . . and we become servants to the choices we make.

Every life, including yours, is a tapestry of choices. And the quality of your life depends, to a surprising extent, on the quality of the choices you make.

> A tranquil heart is life
> to the body,
> but jealousy is
> rottenness to the bones.
>
> Proverbs 14:30 Holman CSB

Would you like to enjoy a life of abundance and significance? If so, you must make choices that are pleasing to God.

From the instant you wake up in the morning until the moment you nod off to sleep at night, you make lots of decisions: decisions about the things you do, decisions about the words you speak, and decisions about the thoughts you choose to think. Today and every day, it's up to you (and only you) to make wise choices, choices that enhance your life and build a stronger relationship with the Creator. After all, He deserves your best . . . and so do you.

## Great Ideas About...
# Contentment

The life of strain is difficult. The life of inner peace—
a life that comes from a positive attitude—
is the easiest type of existence.

*Norman Vincent Peale*

If God chooses to remain silent, faith is content.

*Ruth Bell Graham*

Contentment is something we learn by adhering to the basics—
cultivating a growing relationship with Jesus Christ, living daily,
and knowing that Christ strengthens us for every challenge.

*Charles Stanley*

The happiness which brings enduring worth to life is not
the superficial happiness that is dependent on circumstances.
It is the happiness and contentment that fills the soul in
the midst of the most distressing of circumstances.

*Billy Graham*

True contentment comes from godliness in the heart,
not from wealth in the hand.

*Warren Wiersbe*

*But godliness with contentment is great gain.*
*For we brought nothing into the world, and we can take*
*nothing out of it. But if we have food and clothing,*
*we will be content with that.*

1 Timothy 6:6-8 NIV

## Today's Tip

Every major failure in life—whether it's related to love, health,
money, or anything else—every major failure is simply
the result of a lot of little failures along the way that were
never attended to. Little failures add up if you let them . . .
so don't let them.

## Your Thoughts

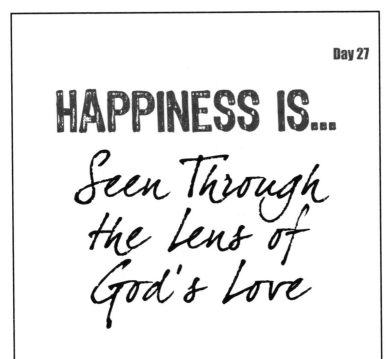

# HAPPINESS IS...

*Seen Through the Lens of God's Love*

And we know that all things work together for good
to them that love God, to them who are
the called according to his purpose.

*Romans 8:28 KJV*

Happiness is learning to live beyond the opinions of people, and learning to see yourself from God's point of view. People will always have opinions. That's the way people are. But the most important thing for you is God's opinion of you. Every other opinion is secondary.

God's love for you is bigger and better than you can imagine. In fact, God's love is far too big to comprehend (in this lifetime). But this much we know: God loves you so much that He sent His Son, Jesus, to come to this earth and die for you. And, when you accepted Jesus into your heart, God gave you a gift that is more precious than gold: the gift of eternal life. Now, precisely because you are a wondrous creation treasured by God, a question presents itself: What will you do in response to God's love? Will you ignore it or embrace it? Will you return it or neglect it? The decision, of course, is yours and yours alone.

> The unfailing love of the LORD never ends!
>
> Lamentations 3:22 NLT

When you embrace God's love, you are forever changed. When you embrace God's love, you feel differently about yourself, your neighbors, and your world. When you embrace God's love, you share His message and you obey His commandments.

When you accept the Father's gift of grace, you are blessed here on earth and throughout all eternity. So do yourself a favor right now: accept God's love with open arms. When you do, your life will be changed today, tomorrow, and forever.

## Great Ideas About...
# God's Love

Being loved by Him whose opinion matters most gives us
the security to risk loving, too—even loving ourselves.

*Gloria Gaither*

There is no pit so deep that God's love is not deeper still.

*Corrie ten Boom*

Love is not something God does; love is something God is.

*Beth Moore*

When once we are assured that God is good,
then there can be nothing left to fear.

*Hannah Whitall Smith*

Though our feelings come and go, His love for us does not.
It is not wearied by our sins, or our indifference; and, therefore,
it is quite relentless in its determination that we shall be cured
of those sins, at whatever cost to us, at whatever cost to Him.

*C. S. Lewis*

*But the love of the LORD remains forever with those who fear him.
His salvation extends to the children's children of those who are
faithful to his covenant, of those who obey his commandments!*

*Psalm 103:17-18 NLT*

*Praise him, all you people of the earth, for he loves us with unfailing
love; the faithfulness of the LORD endures forever. Praise the LORD!*

*Psalm 117 NLT*

## Today's Tip

The most important opinion about your life is God's opinion.
Remember that in God's eyes, you're precious . . .
and it's His perspective that really matters.

*Your Thoughts*

_____

_____

_____

_____

_____

_____

_____

_____

_____

# HAPPINESS IS...

*Having Hope for the Future, Having Faith in God*

For I know the thoughts that I think toward you,
says the LORD, thoughts of peace and not of evil, to give you
a future and a hope. Then you will call upon Me
and go and pray to Me, and I will listen to you.

*Jeremiah 29:11-12 NKJV*

The self-fulfilling prophecy is alive, well, and living at your house. If you trust God and have faith in the future, your optimistic beliefs will give you direction and motivation. That's one reason that you should never lose hope, but certainly not the only reason. The primary reason that you, as a believer, should never lose hope, is because of God's unfailing promises.

> May the God of hope fill you with all joy and peace as you trust in him, so that you may overflow with hope by the power of the Holy Spirit.
>
> Romans 15:13 NIV

Make no mistake about it: thoughts are powerful things—your thoughts have the power to lift you up or to hold you down. When you acquire the habit of hopeful thinking, you will have acquired a powerful tool for improving your life. So if you find yourself falling into the spiritual traps of worry and discouragement, be sure to redirect your thoughts. And if you fall into the terrible habit of negative thinking, think again. After all, God's Word teaches us that Christ can overcome every difficulty. And when God makes a promise, He keeps it.

## Great Ideas About...
# Hope

The grand essentials to happiness in this life are
something to do, something to love, and something to hope for.

*Joseph Addison*

Hope looks for the good in people, opens doors for people,
discovers what can be done to help, lights a candle,
does not yield to cynicism. Hope sets people free.

*Barbara Johnson*

Live for today, but hold your hands open to tomorrow.
Anticipate the future and its changes with joy.
There is a seed of God's love in every event, every circumstance,
every unpleasant situation in which you may find yourself.

*Barbara Johnson*

Never yield to gloomy anticipation. Place your hope
and confidence in God. He has no record of failure.

*Mrs. Charles E. Cowman*

Be hopeful! For tomorrow has never happened before.

*Robert Schuller*

*Let us hold on to the confession of our hope without wavering,*
*for He who promised is faithful.*

*Hebrews 10:23 Holman CSB*

*For I hope in You, O LORD; You will answer, O Lord my God.*

*Psalm 38:15 NASB*

## Today's Tip

Jesus came to give us abundant life, to change the quality
of our existence. Our job, of course, is to obey, to pray, to work,
and to accept His abundance with open arms.

*Your Thoughts*

# HAPPINESS IS...

## The Right Kind of Input

*Always be happy. Never stop praying.*
*Give thanks whatever happens.*
*That is what God wants for you in Christ Jesus.*

1 Thessalonians 5:16-18 ICB

I f you want to be happy, if you want to be healthy, if you want to be prosperous, if you want to have a good marriage, if you want to have good relationships, if you want to have peace of mind, how can you do it? Well a great place to start is by making sure that you're putting the right kind of thoughts into your mind. If you want to enjoy better results, you'll need to improve the quality of the input that you feed into your brain. And the sooner you start sending the right kind of messages in your mind, the sooner you'll begin producing the results you want.

> Obey God and
> be at peace with him;
> this is the way to
> happiness.
>
> Job 22:21 NCV

Human nature being what it is, you'll be tempted to think—and to behave—in undisciplined ways. But you must resist that temptation. Otherwise, when crisis comes, you'll be tempted to imagine the worst, to plan for the worst, to expect the worst, and to live down to your expectations.

So, do yourself and your loved ones a big-league favor: fill your mind with the right kind of input. When you do, your output will, more often than not, take care of itself.

## Great Ideas About...
# Happiness

Each one of us is responsible for our own happiness.
If we choose to allow ourselves to become miserable
and unhappy, the problem is ours, not someone else's.

*Joyce Meyer*

Happiness is when what you think, what you say,
and what you do are in harmony.

*Gandhi*

Act as if you were already happy,
and that will tend to make you happy.

*Dale Carnegie*

Pleasure-seeking is a barren business;
happiness is never found till we have the grace
to stop looking for it and to give our attention
to persons and matters external to ourselves.

*J. I. Packer*

*I will praise you, LORD, with all my heart.*
*I will tell all the miracles you have done. I will be happy because*
*of you; God Most High, I will sing praises to your name.*

Psalm 9:1-2 NCV

*How happy are those who can live in your house,*
*always singing your praises.*
*How happy are those who are strong in the Lord . . . .*

Psalm 84:4-5 NLT

## Today's Tip

The best day to be happy is "today."
Don't spend your whole life in the waiting room.

*Your Thoughts*

_____

_____

_____

_____

_____

_____

_____

_____

_____

# HAPPINESS IS...

*Walking with God's Son*

For God so loved the world that He gave
His only begotten Son, that whoever believes in Him
should not perish but have everlasting life.

*John 3:16 NKJV*

Since He walked this earth over two thousand years ago, Jesus has called upon people of every generation (and that includes you) to follow in His footsteps. And God's Word promises that when you follow in Christ's footsteps, you will experience abundance, happiness, and joy.

Who will you choose to walk with today? Will you walk with shortsighted people who honor the ways of the world, or will you walk with the Son of God? Jesus walks with you. Are you walking with Him? Hopefully, you will choose to walk with Him today and every day of your life.

> And when he had
> spoken this,
> he saith unto him,
> Follow me.
>
> John 21:19 KJV

God doesn't want you to have a run-of-the-mill, follow-the-crowd kind of existence. God wants you to be a "new creation" through Him. And that's exactly what you should want for yourself, too. God deserves your extreme enthusiasm; the world deserves it; and you deserve the experience of sharing it. So what, neighbor, are you waiting for?

## Great Ideas About...
# Jesus

Think of this—we may live together with Him here and now,
a daily walking with Him who loved us and gave Himself for us.

*Elisabeth Elliot*

To walk out of His will is to walk into nowhere.

*C. S. Lewis*

When we truly walk with God throughout our day,
life slowly starts to fall into place.

*Bill Hybels*

Being a Christian is more than just an instantaneous conversion;
it is like a daily process whereby you grow to be
more and more like Christ.

*Billy Graham*

Happiness is the byproduct of a life that is lived in the will of
God. When we humbly serve others, walk in God's path of
holiness, and do what He tells us, then we will enjoy happiness.

*Warren Wiersbe*

*Whoever is not willing to carry the cross and follow me is not worthy of me. Those who try to hold on to their lives will give up true life. Those who give up their lives for me will hold on to true life.*

Matthew 10:38-39 NCV

*If anyone would come after me, he must deny himself and take up his cross and follow me.*

Mark 8:34 NIV

## Today's Tip

You don't have to be perfect to follow in Christ's footsteps.
Jesus doesn't expect your perfection—
He expects your participation.

*Your Thoughts*

_____

_____

_____

_____

_____

_____

_____

_____

*Thinking*
*About*
*Your Values*

**W**hat things are really important to you—God, family, church, health, wealth, happiness? Please take the time to write down 16 values like these—at least 16 things that form the foundation of your life. Then go back over the list, look things over, and prioritize these values in the approximate order of their importance to you. Finally, refer back to this list often, especially when you're making critical decisions.

Peace comes naturally when your values and your actions are in agreement. Yet, far too many people forfeit happiness because their values and their actions are in conflict. In order to avoid this mistake, you should know precisely what your values are, and you should conduct yourself accordingly.

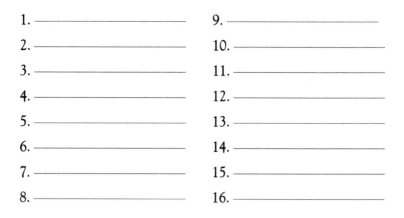

1. ——————————————

2. ——————————————

3. ——————————————

4. ——————————————

5. ——————————————

6. ——————————————

7. ——————————————

8. ——————————————

9. ——————————————

10. ——————————————

11. ——————————————

12. ——————————————

13. ——————————————

14. ——————————————

15. ——————————————

16. ——————————————

# Bible Verses
to Consider

# Asking God

So I say to you, ask, and it will be given to you; seek,
and you will find; knock, and it will be opened to you.
For everyone who asks receives, and he who seeks finds,
and to him who knocks it will be opened.

*Luke 11:9-10 NKJV*

Do not worry about anything, but pray and ask God
for everything you need, always giving thanks.

*Philippians 4:6 NCV*

Verily, verily, I say unto you, He that believeth on me,
the works that I do shall he do also; and greater works than these
shall he do; because I go unto my Father. And whatsoever ye shall ask
in my name, that will I do, that the Father may be glorified in
the Son. If ye shall ask any thing in my name, I will do it.

*John 14:12-14 KJV*

You did not choose me, but I chose you and appointed you
to go and bear fruit—fruit that will last.
Then the Father will give you whatever you ask in my name.

*John 15:16 NIV*

*You do not have,
because you do not
ask God.*

James 4:2 NIV

# Courage

The LORD himself goes before you and will be with you;
he will never leave you nor forsake you.
Do not be afraid; do not be discouraged.

*Deuteronomy 31:8 NIV*

So do not fear, for I am with you; do not be dismayed,
for I am your God. I will strengthen you and help you;
I will uphold you with my righteous right hand.

*Isaiah 41:10 NIV*

Peace I leave with you, my peace I give unto you:
not as the world giveth, give I unto you.
Let not your heart be troubled, neither let it be afraid.

*John 14:27 KJV*

In thee, O LORD, do I put my trust;
let me never be put into confusion.

*Psalm 71:1 KJV*

# Diligence

Now we want each of you to demonstrate
the same diligence for the final realization of your hope,
so that you won't become lazy, but imitators of those
who inherit the promises through faith and perseverance.

*Hebrews 6:11-12 Holman CSB*

He was diligent in every deed that he began in the service
of God's temple, in the law and in the commandment,
in order to seek his God, and he prospered.

*2 Chronicles 31:21 Holman CSB*

Idle hands make one poor, but diligent hands bring riches.

*Proverbs 10:4 Holman CSB*

But as for you, be strong; don't be discouraged,
for your work has a reward.

*2 Chronicles 15:7 Holman CSB*

I have fought the good fight, I have finished the race,
I have kept the faith.

*2 Timothy 4:7 Holman CSB*

# God's Guidance

The Lord says, "I will make you wise and show you where to go.
I will guide you and watch over you."

*Psalm 32:8 NCV*

The true children of God are those who let God's Spirit lead them.

*Romans 8:14 NCV*

Lord, You light my lamp; my God illuminates my darkness.

*Psalm 18:28 Holman CSB*

In all your ways acknowledge Him, and He shall direct your paths.

*Proverbs 3:6 NKJV*

Every morning he wakes me. He teaches me to listen like a student.
The Lord God helps me learn . . . .

*Isaiah 50:4-5 NCV*

# God's Timing

To everything there is a season,
a time for every purpose under heaven.

*Ecclesiastes 3:1 NKJV*

This is what the LORD says:
"In the time of my favor I will answer you,
and in the day of salvation I will help you . . . .

*Isaiah 49:8 NIV*

Humble yourselves, therefore, under God's mighty hand,
that he may lift you up in due time.

*1 Peter 5:6 NIV*

From one man he made every nation of men, that they
should inhabit the whole earth; and he determined the times set
for them and the exact places where they should live.

*Acts 17:26 NIV*

Wait for the LORD; be strong and take heart
and wait for the LORD.

*Psalm 27:14 NIV*

# The Golden Rule

*Just as you want others to do for you, do the same for them.*

*Luke 6:31 Holman CSB*

*Let us not become weary in doing good,*
*for at the proper time we will reap a harvest if we do not give up.*

*Galatians 6:9 NIV*

*Each of you should look not only to your own interests,*
*but also to the interest of others.*

*Philippians 2:4 NIV*

*Carry each other's burdens, and in this way you will*
*fulfill the law of Christ.*

*Galatians 6:2 NIV*

*See that no one renders evil for evil to anyone,*
*but always pursue what is good both for yourselves and for all.*

*1 Thessalonians 5:15 NKJV*

# *Maturity*

*Don't become so well-adjusted to your culture that you fit into it*
*without even thinking. Instead, fix your attention on God.*
*You'll be changed from the inside out. Readily recognize what*
*he wants from you, and quickly respond to it. Unlike the culture*
*around you, always dragging you down to its level of immaturity,*
*God brings the best out of you, develops well-formed maturity in you.*

*Romans 12:2 MSG*

*Let the wise listen and add to their learning,*
*and let the discerning get guidance.*

*Proverbs 1:5 NIV*

*He who began a good work in you will carry it on*
*to completion until the day of Christ Jesus.*

*Philippians 1:6 NIV*

*Take my yoke upon you and learn from me . . . .*

*Matthew 11:29 NIV*

*But endurance must do its complete work,*
*so that you may be mature and complete, lacking nothing.*

*James 1:4 Holman CSB*

# *Missions*

But you will receive power when the Holy Spirit has come upon you,
and you will be My witnesses in Jerusalem,
in all Judea and Samaria, and to the ends of the earth.

*Acts 1:8 Holman CSB*

After this the Lord appointed 70 others, and He sent them ahead
of Him in pairs to every town and place where He Himself was about
to go. He told them: "The harvest is abundant, but the workers are
few. Therefore, pray to the Lord of the harvest to send out workers
into His harvest. Now go; I'm sending you
out like lambs among wolves."

*Luke 10:1-3 Holman CSB*

Then He said to them,
"Go into all the world and preach the gospel to the whole creation."

*Mark 16:15 Holman CSB*

Jesus sent out these 12 after giving them instructions:
"Don't take the road leading to other nations, and don't enter any
Samaritan town. Instead, go to the lost sheep of the house of Israel.
As you go, announce this: 'The kingdom of heaven has come near.'
Heal the sick, raise the dead, cleanse the lepers, drive out demons.
You have received free of charge; give free of charge."

*Matthew 10:5-8 Holman CSB*

What I tell you in the dark, speak in the light. What you hear in a whisper, proclaim on the housetops.

*Matthew 10:27 Holman CSB*

# New Beginnings

And He who sits on the throne said,
"Behold, I am making all things new."

*Revelation 21:5 NASB*


Create in me a pure heart, O God,
and renew a steadfast spirit within me.

*Psalm 51:10 NIV*


. . . inwardly we are being renewed day by day.

*2 Corinthians 4:16 NIV*


I will give you a new heart and put a new spirit in you . . . .

*Ezekiel 36:26 NIV*


Remember ye not the former things,
neither consider the things of old. Behold, I will do a new thing . . . .

*Isaiah 43:18-19 KJV*

# Optimism

*But if we look forward to something we don't have yet,*
*we must wait patiently and confidently.*

*Romans 8:25 NLT*

*Make me hear joy and gladness.*

*Psalm 51:8 NKJV*

*My cup runs over.*
*Surely goodness and mercy shall follow me all the days of my life;*
*and I will dwell in the house of the LORD forever.*

*Psalm 23:5-6 NKJV*

*I can do everything through him that gives me strength.*

*Philippians 4:13 NIV*

*For God has not given us a spirit of fear,*
*but of power and of love and of a sound mind.*

*2 Timothy 1:7 NLT*

# *Perseverance*

*Thanks be to God! He gives us the victory through our Lord Jesus Christ. Therefore, my dear brothers, stand firm. Let nothing move you. Always give yourselves fully to the work of the Lord, because you know that your labor in the Lord is not in vain.*

*1 Corinthians 15:57-58 NIV*

*I do not consider myself yet to have taken hold of it. But one thing I do: Forgetting what is behind and straining toward what is ahead, I press on toward the goal to win the prize for which God has called me heavenward in Christ Jesus.*

*Philippians 3:13-14 NIV*

*Let us not become weary in doing good, for at the proper time we will reap a harvest if we do not give up.*

*Galatians 6:9 NIV*

*You need to persevere so that when you have done the will of God, you will receive what he has promised.*

*Hebrews 10:36 NIV*

*I have fought a good fight, I have finished my course, I have kept the faith.*

*2 Timothy 4:7 KJV*

# Problems

Let not your heart be troubled: ye believe in God, believe also in me.

*John 14:1 KJV*

People who do what is right may have many problems,
but the Lord will solve them all.

*Psalm 34:19 NCV*

Be joyful because you have hope.
Be patient when trouble comes, and pray at all times.

*Romans 12:12 NCV*

I have told you these things, so that in me you may have peace.
In this world you will have trouble.
But take heart! I have overcome the world.

*John 16:33 NIV*

When troubles come and all these awful things happen to you,
in future days you will come back to God, your God, and listen
obediently to what he says. God, your God, is above all
a compassionate God. In the end he will not abandon you,
he won't bring you to ruin, he won't forget the covenant
with your ancestors which he swore to them.

*Deuteronomy 4:30-31 MSG*

# Renewal

But may the God of all grace, who called us to
His eternal glory by Christ Jesus, after you have suffered a while,
perfect, establish, strengthen, and settle you.

*1 Peter 5:10 NKJV*

Finally, brothers, rejoice. Be restored, be encouraged,
be of the same mind, be at peace, and the God of love
and peace will be with you.

*2 Corinthians 13:11 Holman CSB*

But those who wait on the LORD Shall renew their strength;
They shall mount up with wings like eagles,
They shall run and not be weary, They shall walk and not faint.

*Isaiah 40:31 NKJV*

Therefore if anyone is in Christ, he is a new creature;
the old things passed away; behold, new things have come.

*2 Corinthians 5:17 Holman CSB*

You are being renewed in the spirit of your minds;
you put on the new man, the one created according to God's likeness
in righteousness and purity of the truth.

*Ephesians 4:23-24 Holman CSB*

I will give you
a new heart and put
a new spirit within you.

*Ezekiel 36:26 Holman CSB*

# Self-worth

*For You have made him a little lower than the angels,*
*And You have crowned him with glory and honor.*

Psalm 8:5 NKJV

*How happy are those whose way is blameless,*
*who live according to the law of the LORD! Happy are those*
*who keep His decrees and seek Him with all their heart.*

Psalm 119:1-2 Holman CSB

*Happy is the one whose help is the God of Jacob,*
*whose hope is in the LORD his God.*

Psalm 146:5 Holman CSB

*If God is for us, who is against us?*

Romans 8:31 Holman CSB

*Finally, brethren, whatever things are true,*
*whatever things are noble, whatever things are just,*
*whatever things are pure, whatever things are lovely,*
*whatever things are of good report, if there is any virtue*
*and if there is anything praiseworthy—*
*meditate on these things.*

Philippians 4:8 NKJV

# Spiritual Growth

*For this reason we also, since the day we heard it, do not cease to pray for you, and to ask that you may be filled with the knowledge of His will in all wisdom and spiritual understanding . . . .*

*Colossians 1:9 NKJV*

*So let us stop going over the basics of Christianity again and again. Let us go on instead and become mature in our understanding.*

*Hebrews 6:1 NLT*

*Run away from infantile indulgence.*
*Run after mature righteousness—faith, love, peace—*
*joining those who are in honest and serious prayer before God.*

*2 Timothy 2:22 MSG*

*For You, O God, have tested us; You have refined us as silver is refined. You brought us into the net; You laid affliction on our backs. You have caused men to ride over our heads; we went through fire and through water; but You brought us out to rich fulfillment.*

*Psalm 66:10-12 NKJV*

*Know the love of Christ which surpasses knowledge, that you may be filled up to all the fullness of God.*

*Ephesians 3:19 NASB*

# Worship

*But the hour cometh, and now is, when the true worshippers*
*shall worship the Father in spirit and in truth:*
*for the Father seeketh such to worship him.*

*John 4:23 KJV*

*Then saith Jesus unto him, Get thee hence, Satan: for it is written,*
*Thou shalt worship the Lord thy God, and him only shalt thou serve.*

*Matthew 4:10 KJV*

*Blessed are they which do hunger and thirst after righteousness:*
*for they shall be filled.*

*Matthew 5:6 KJV*

*Worship the LORD with gladness. Come before him, singing with joy.*
*Acknowledge that the LORD is God! He made us, and we are his.*
*We are his people, the sheep of his pasture.*

*Psalm 100:2-3 NLT*

*And every day they devoted themselves to meeting together in the*
*temple complex, and broke bread from house to house.*
*They ate their food with gladness and simplicity of heart,*
*praising God and having favor with all the people.*
*And every day the Lord added those being saved to them.*

*Acts 2:46-47 Holman CSB*

Happy are those
who hear the joyful
call to worship,
for they will walk
in the light of
your presence, LORD.

Psalm 89:15 NLT